BAPTISM GOD'S WAY

Everything
God has to say
about baptism

Everything
GOD HAS TO SAY
about baptism

Baptism GOD'S WAY

- THANE HAYHURST -

Baptism God's Way

ISBN 979-8-9901676-0-5

First paperback edition 2024

Book design by Lindsay Armistead Williams

Printed by Amazon.com, Inc.

To my wife, Julie, whom I baptized

in the Mediterranean Sea

on our honeymoon.

my baptism

NAME

was baptized by

NAME OF PERSON WHO BAPTIZED YOU

on

DATE

at

LOCATION

If you want to learn everything God teaches about a subject, a Topical Bible Study is the best approach.

Baptism God's Way is a Topical Bible Study.
It contains all the verses in the Bible about baptism[1].
It helps you quickly and easily study and learn directly from God's Word. We've also included some questions to guide your study.

---

[1] Some stories in Matthew are repeated in Mark chapters 1 & 11, Luke chapters 3 & 20, and John chapter 1, but those duplications are not included.

contents

INTRODUCTION

THE GOSPELS

THE ACTS

introduction

– BAPTISM –

What does the Bible say?

This is a collection of all the verses in the Bible that mention baptism.

A lot has been said and written about baptism, but God's word is the best teacher of the full truth on any spiritual matter. You can easily read and understand God's instructions on baptism in the same time it would take you to read another book or article. The difference is that this book doesn't tell you what to believe. It simply lists the Scriptures so you can read what God says for yourself. In Acts 17:11 we are instructed not to simply believe what someone tells us, but to study the Scriptures for ourselves to see if what they say is true. This document makes that process easy for you as it relates to the topic of baptism.

THE VALUE OF A TOPICAL STUDY

The Scriptures aren't like other books whose authors group information into neat little chapters for us. The Bible doesn't contain a chapter on love, or a chapter on Jesus, or a chapter on baptism. In fact, the Bible doesn't contain any single chapter that covers all God has to say on any topic. Each biblical topic is woven throughout the various books of the Bible.

Therefore, in order to gain complete understanding on a subject as God intended, we have to search for it. This study method is called a "Topical Study." A Topical Study involves collecting all the passages related to a topic and then studying them all together. This is the only way to arrive at a full understanding of a biblical subject. That is what we have done for you here. All of the verses dealing with baptism are gathered here[1] for you to read and study and draw your own conclusions.

THREE CAUTIONS

1. Don't take shortcuts. Some people try to develop doctrines based on only some of the verses related to a particular topic. Over the centuries, people have done this with nearly every biblical subject, including baptism. That approach will almost always lead to a dangerously inaccurate set of conclusions. It is much wiser to study all—not a few, or some, or even most, but all—the verses on a topic before forming irreversible conclusions on the subject. Take the time to discover wonderful insights into what is written, and what is not written, about each topic. Test your early conclusions by revisiting each verse on the topic to make sure your current viewpoint doesn't contradict even one passage. If your opinion of the moment does seem to contradict a verse or two, rethink your stance and see how you can accurately incorporate all the verses God gave us on the topic. (c.f. Galatians 1:8-9 and Revelation 22:18-19)

[1] Some stories in Matthew are repeated in Mark chapters 1 & 11, Luke chapters 3 & 20, and John chapter 1, but those duplications are not included.

2. Be careful not to bring old ideas into your new study, even if those viewpoints were taught to you by people you love dearly, trust implicitly and respect wholeheartedly. Certainly, keep their views in mind, but God gave you a brain, too, and He may reveal something to you that you haven't seen or heard before. Just read the verses and see what God says to you through His Word.

3. Summarizing things is essential to gaining a clear understanding, but try not to over-simplify or humanize the spiritual meanings and intentions of a passage. For example, some people define baptism as a "public display of an inward change." That is sort of true, as baptism is about repentance and submission to Christ, which are definitely inward changes in our hearts, but there is more to baptism than that. Nowhere does Scripture describe or even imply that baptism is a public display of these changes. In actuality, there is more than one example of people being baptized with very few, or maybe no, witnesses. Also, the words "inward change" unnecessarily summarize and diminish the more powerful and complete meaning that "repentance and submission to God" describes. But don't take my word for it. Read the Scriptures for yourself to see what is and isn't true on this most important and intriguing topic.

WHAT'S INCLUDED IN THIS STUDY

Each section of this Study includes questions or comments designed to provoke thought and help you draw your own conclusions. Feel free to use these if you find them helpful or ignore them if you prefer to think through the passages on your own.

YOUR CURRENT UNDERSTANDING

Before you get started, take a couple of minutes to write down your answers to these three questions.

1. What do you currently understand the purpose and meaning of baptism to be?

   ____

   ____

   ____

2. Does it matter if a person is baptized by immersion, sprinkling, or pouring? How do you know?

   ____

   ____

   ____

3. How do we get our sins forgiven? Obviously, Jesus paid the price on the cross, but what do we have to do, if anything?

   ____

   ____

   ____

Some stories in Matthew are repeated in Mark chapters 1 & 11, Luke chapters 3 & 20, and John chapter 1, but those duplications are not included.

I pray you enjoy learning about baptism through this study.

– *Thane Hayhurst*

the gospels

A collection of all the passages in
the Gospels that mention baptism.

Matthew 3

5 People went out to him [John the Baptist] from Jerusalem and all Judea
and the whole region of the Jordan. 6 Confessing their sins, they were baptized by him in the Jordan River.

7 But when he saw many of the Pharisees and Sadducees coming to where
he was baptizing, he said to them: "You brood of vipers! Who warned you
to flee from the coming wrath? 8 Produce fruit in keeping with repentance.
9 And do not think you can say to yourselves, `We have Abraham as our
father.' I tell you that out of these stones God can raise up children for
Abraham. 10 The axe is already at the root of the trees, and every tree that
does not produce good fruit will be cut down and thrown into the fire.

11 "I baptize you with [or in] water for repentance. But after me will come
one who is more powerful than I, whose sandals I am not fit to carry. He
will baptize you with the Holy Spirit and with fire. 12 His winnowing fork is
in his hand, and he will clear his threshing-floor, gathering his wheat into
the barn and burning up the chaff with unquenchable fire."

13 Then Jesus came from Galilee to the Jordan to be baptized by John.
14 But John tried to deter him, saying, "I need to be baptized by you, and
do you come to me?"

15 Jesus replied, "Let it be so now; it is proper for us to do this to fulfill all
righteousness." Then John consented.

16 As soon as Jesus was baptized, he went up out of the water. At that
moment heaven was opened, and he saw the Spirit of God descending like
a dove and lighting on him. 17 And a voice from heaven said, "This is my
Son, whom I love; with him I am well pleased."

1. What did the people do as they were about to be baptized? (v.6)

2. Should we keep this practice today? Why/Why not?

3. People are baptized in what substance? (v.11)

4. When did Jesus receive the Spirit of God (Holy Spirit)? (v.16)

5. If Jesus baptizes with the Holy Spirit and with fire, how does that fit with other verses where we are instructed to be baptized in water?

6. List any other interesting points you learned from this passage. *Only write what this passage says, not what other passages say.*

Matthew 21

23 Jesus entered the temple courts, and, while he was teaching, the chief
priests and the elders of the people came to him. "By what authority are
you doing these things?" they asked. "And who gave you this authority?"

24 Jesus replied, "I will also ask you one question. If you answer me, I will
tell you by what authority I am doing these things. 25 John's baptism —
where did it come from? Was it from heaven, or from men?"

They discussed it among themselves and said, "If we say, 'From heaven',
he will ask, 'Then why didn't you believe him?' 26 But if we say, 'From
men' — we are afraid of the people, for they all hold that John was a
prophet." 27 So they answered Jesus, "We don't know."

Then he said, "Neither will I tell you by what authority I am doing these things.

1. Whose idea is baptism: Ours or God's?

Matthew 28

18 Then Jesus came to them and said, "All authority in heaven and on earth
has been given to me. 19 Therefore go and make disciples of all nations,
baptizing them in [or into] the name of the Father and of the Son and
of the Holy Spirit, 20 and teaching them to obey everything I have commanded you. And surely I am with you always, to the very end of the age."

1. These are Jesus' final instructions to his disciples. List the three things He told them to do.

   a. ______________________________

   b. ______________________________

   c. ______________________________

2. How important do you think Jesus might have thought baptism is by what you read in this verse? Why?

   ____

   ____

   ____

   ____

   ____

   ____

   ____

Mark 1

4 And so John came, baptizing in the desert region and preaching a baptism
of repentance for the forgiveness of sins. 5 The whole Judean countryside
and all the people of Jerusalem went out to him. Confessing their sins, they
were baptized by him in the Jordan River.

1. What was the purpose of John's baptism? (v.4)

____

____

2. Does this mesh with your current understanding of the purpose of baptism?

____

3. Why do you think they were baptized "in" the Jordan River, not simply "near" or "beside" the river?

____

____

____

4. This passage talks about repentance, confessing sins, baptism, and forgiveness of sins. Analyzing only this passage, what does it imply the relationship is between these four topics?

____

____

____

____

____

____

____

Mark 10

35 Then James and John, the sons of Zebedee, came to him. "Teacher," they said, "we want you to do for us whatever we ask."

36 "What do you want me to do for you?" he asked.

37 They replied, "Let one of us sit at your right and the other at your left in your glory."

38 "You don't know what you are asking," Jesus said. "Can you drink the cup I drink or be baptized with the baptism I am baptized with?"

39 "We can," they answered.

Jesus said to them, "You will drink the cup I drink and be baptized with the
baptism I am baptized with, 40 but to sit at my right or left is not for me to
grant. These places belong to those for whom they have been prepared."

1. Is this passage talking about a different baptism than what we do today? Explore both the 'yes' and 'no' sides to see what you can figure out.

Mark 16

14 Later Jesus appeared to the Eleven as they were eating; he rebuked them
for their lack of faith and their stubborn refusal to believe those who had
seen him after he had risen. 15 He said to them, "Go into all the world and
preach the good news to all creation. 16 Whoever believes and is baptized
will be saved, but whoever does not believe will be condemned.

1. According to this verse, what does Jesus state are the two things one must do to be saved?

   a. ______________________________

   b. ______________________________

2. Other verses talk of other things we must do to be saved. How do you reconcile all these seemingly contradictory or overlapping declarations of salvation?

   ____

   ____

   ____

   ____

   ____

3. Why does the writer list two factors — belief and baptism —to be saved, but only one factor — unbelief — for someone to be condemned?

   ____

   ____

   ____

   ____

   ____

Luke 3

3 He [John the Baptist] went into all the country around the Jordan,
preaching a baptism of repentance for the forgiveness of sins.

1. What does this verse say our part is in being baptized?

____

2. What does this verse say God's gift is to those who are baptized?

____

3. Can someone go to heaven without having their sins forgiven?

____

____

4. Baptism is the only thing a believer is involved in that we don't do for ourselves. We believe in God ourselves. We confess our sins ourselves. We pray ourselves. We repent ourselves. We acknowledge Jesus as Lord ourselves. We do good deeds ourselves, etc. But someone else baptizes us. Why do you think that is?

____

____

____

____

____

____

____

____

____

Luke 7

29 All the people, even the tax collectors, when they heard Jesus' words,
acknowledged that God's way was right, because they had been baptized
by John. 30 But the Pharisees and experts in the law rejected God's purpose
for themselves, because they had not been baptized by John.

Luke 12

49 "I have come to bring fire on the earth, and how I wish it were already
kindled! 50 But I have a baptism to undergo, and how distressed I am until
it is completed! 51 Do you think I came to bring peace on earth? No, I tell
you, but division. 52 From now on there will be five in one family divided
against each other, three against two and two against three.

1. Why would having been baptized by John make any difference in whether people accepted Jesus' teachings?

2. What is Jesus referring to in Luke 12 about a baptism He has to undergo? Remember, He was already baptized by John about three years prior to this.

John 3

1 Now there was a man of the Pharisees named Nicodemus, a member of
the Jewish ruling council. 2 He came to Jesus at night and said, "Rabbi,
we know you are a teacher who has come from God. For no-one could
perform the miraculous signs you are doing if God were not with him."

3 In reply Jesus declared, "I tell you the truth, no-one can see the kingdom
of God unless he is born again."

4 "How can a man be born when he is old?" Nicodemus asked. "Surely he
cannot enter a second time into his mother's womb to be born!"

5 Jesus answered, "I tell you the truth, no-one can enter the kingdom of
God unless he is born of water and the Spirit. 6 Flesh gives birth to flesh,
but the Spirit [or but spirit] gives birth to spirit. 7 You should not be sur-
prised at my saying, `You must be born again.' 8 The wind blows wherever
it pleases. You hear its sound, but you cannot tell where it comes from or
where it is going. So it is with everyone born of the Spirit."

1. What does "born again" mean?

____

____

2. What does "born again" NOT mean?

____

____

3. Are "born again" and "born of water and the Spirit" the same thing?

____

____

4. How did you come to that conclusion?

____

____

____

Clue: Refer to all the other verses on the subject and use a combination of the Scientific Method and the process of elimination to determine the true meaning

5. According to this passage, who does and who does not get to enter the kingdom of God?

____

____

____

____

John 3

22 After this, Jesus and his disciples went out into the Judean countryside,
where he spent some time with them, and baptized. 23 Now John also was
baptizing at Aenon near Salim, because there was plenty of water, and
people were constantly coming to be baptized.

~

26 John's disciples came to John and said to him, "Rabbi, that man who
was with you on the other side of the Jordan — the one you testified about
— well, he is baptizing, and everyone is going to him."

27 To this John replied, "A man can receive only what is given him from
heaven. 28 You yourselves can testify that I said, 'I am not the Christ but
am sent ahead of him.' 29 The bride belongs to the bridegroom. The
friend who attends the bridegroom waits and listens for him, and is full of
joy when he hears the bridegroom's voice. That joy is mine, and it is now
complete. 30 He must become greater; I must become less.

John 4

1 The Pharisees heard that Jesus was gaining and baptizing more disciples
than John, 2 although in fact it was not Jesus who baptized, but his disciples.

John 10

40 Then Jesus went back across the Jordan to the place where John had
been baptizing in the early days.

1. If baptism could be done by sprinkling or pouring, would a lot of water be needed, even for large crowds?

2. Why do you think Jesus let His disciples baptize everyone instead of doing that Himself?

the acts

A collection of all the passages in the Acts that mention baptism.

Acts 1

4 On one occasion, while he [Jesus] was eating with them, he gave them
this command: "Do not leave Jerusalem, but wait for the gift my Father
promised, which you have heard me speak about. 5 For John baptized with
[or in] water, but in a few days you will be baptized with the Holy Spirit."

~

21 Therefore it is necessary to choose one of the men who have been with
us the whole time the Lord Jesus went in and out among us, 22 beginning
from John's baptism to the time when Jesus was taken up from us. For one
of these must become a witness with us of his resurrection."

1. Why did Jesus mention John's baptism when telling the disciples they'd receive the Holy Spirit?

2. Why did the new apostle have to have been around since Jesus' baptism?

Acts 2

This is the first time the gospel is preached after Jesus went back to Heaven.

37 When the people heard this, they were cut to the heart and said to Peter
and the other apostles, "Brothers, what shall we do?"

38 Peter replied, "Repent and be baptized, every one of you, in the name
of Jesus Christ for the forgiveness of your sins. And you will receive the gift
of the Holy Spirit. 39 The promise is for you and your children and for all
who are far off — for all whom the Lord our God will call."

40 With many other words he warned them; and he pleaded with them,
"Save yourselves from this corrupt generation." 41 Those who accepted
his message were baptized, and about three thousand were added to their
number that day.

1. List the two things the people were told to do that day if they believed the gospel Peter just preached to them.

   a. ______________________________

   b. ______________________________

2. What spiritual benefits were granted to those who obeyed these instructions?

   ____

   ____

   ____

   ____

3. According to Peter, to whom does God extend His promise?

   ____

4. What warnings do you think Peter might have shared with the crowd?

   ____

   ____

   ____

   ____

Acts 8

[5] Philip went down to a city in Samaria and proclaimed the Messiah there.
[6] When the crowds heard Philip and saw the signs he performed, they all
paid close attention to what he said.

[12] When they believed Philip as he proclaimed the good news of the kingdom of God and the name of Jesus Christ, they were baptized, both men
and women. [13] Simon himself believed and was baptized. And he followed
Philip everywhere, astonished by the great signs and miracles he saw.

1. In this passage, why did the people choose to be baptized?

Acts 8

27 Philip met an Ethiopian eunuch, an important official in charge of all
the treasury of Candace, queen of the Ethiopians. This man had gone to
Jerusalem to worship, 28 and on his way home was sitting in his chariot
reading the book of Isaiah the prophet. 30 Philip ran up to the chariot and
heard the man reading Isaiah the prophet. "Do you understand what you
are reading?" Philip asked.

31 "How can I," he said, "unless someone explains it to me?" So he invited
Philip to come up and sit with him. 32 The eunuch was reading this passage of Scripture: "He was led like a sheep to the slaughter, and as a lamb
before the shearer is silent, so he did not open his mouth. 33 In his humil-
iation he was deprived of justice. Who can speak of his descendants? For
his life was taken from the earth." [Isaiah 53:7,8]

34 The eunuch asked Philip, "Tell me, please, who is the prophet talking
about, himself or someone else?" 35 Then Philip began with that very passage of Scripture and told him the good news about Jesus.

36 As they travelled along the road, they came to some water and the
eunuch said, "Look, here is water. Why shouldn't I be baptized?"

37 Philip said, "If you believe with all your heart, you may." The eunuch
answered, "I believe that Jesus Christ is the Son of God."

38 And he gave orders to stop the chariot. Then both Philip and the eunuch
went down into the water and Philip baptized him. 39 When they came up
out of the water, the Spirit of the Lord suddenly took Philip away, and the
eunuch did not see him again, but went on his way rejoicing.

1. What does this passage teach us about the mechanics of baptism; before, during and after?

Acts 9

17 Then Ananias went to the house and entered it. Placing his hands on
Saul, he said, "Brother Saul, the Lord — Jesus, who appeared to you on
the road as you were coming here — has sent me so that you may see again
and be filled with the Holy Spirit." 18 Immediately, something like scales
fell from Saul's eyes, and he could see again. He got up and was baptized.

1. How soon was Saul baptized after understanding the truth about Jesus?

____

Acts 10

23 ... Peter started out with [Cornelius' men] and some of the believers
from Joppa. 24 The following day he arrived in Caesarea. Cornelius was
expecting them and had called together his relatives and close friends.
25 As Peter entered the house, Cornelius met him and said ...

33 ... "Now we are all here in the presence of God to listen to everything
the Lord has commanded you to tell us."

34 Then Peter began to speak: "I now realize how true it is that God does
not show favoritism 35 but accepts men from every nation who fear him
and do what is right. 36 You know the message God sent to the people of
Israel, telling the good news of peace through Jesus Christ, who is Lord
of all. 37 You know what has happened throughout Judea, beginning in
Galilee after the baptism that John preached — 38 how God anointed Jesus
of Nazareth with the Holy Spirit and power, and how he went around
doing good and healing all who were under the power of the devil, because
God was with him.

39 "We are witnesses of everything he did in the country of the Jews and
in Jerusalem. They killed him by hanging him on a tree, 40 but God raised
him from the dead on the third day and caused him to be seen.

42 He commanded us to preach to the people and to testify that he is the
one whom God appointed as judge of the living and the dead. 43 All the
prophets testify about him that everyone who believes in him receives forgiveness of sins through his name."

44 While Peter was still speaking these words, the Holy Spirit came on all
who heard the message. 45 The circumcised believers who had come with
Peter were astonished that the gift of the Holy Spirit had been poured
out even on the Gentiles. 46 For they heard them speaking in other lan-
guages [tongues] and praising God. Then Peter said, 47 "Can anyone keep
these people from being baptized with water? They have received the Holy
Spirit just as we have."

48 So he ordered that they be baptized in the name of Jesus Christ. Then
they asked Peter to stay with them for a few days.

1. After God revealed to Peter that He accepted the Gentiles by giving them the Holy Spirit, what was the first thing Peter told them to do? (v. 47)

2. If water baptism wasn't important, why would Peter command it?

Acts 11

Peter is explaining why he met with Cornelius to the believers in Jerusalem.

15 "As I began to speak, the Holy Spirit came on them as he had come on
us at the beginning. 16 Then I remembered what the Lord had said: 'John
baptized with [or in] water, but you will be baptized with the Holy Spirit.'

17 So if God gave them the same gift as he gave us, who believed in the
Lord Jesus Christ, who was I to think that I could oppose God?"

18 When they heard this, they had no further objections and praised God,
saying, "So then, God has granted even the Gentiles repentance unto life."

1. Are there any areas in your life you want to oppose God? List them here.

Acts 13

24 Before the coming of Jesus, John preached repentance and baptism to
all the people of Israel.

1. What does baptism have to do with repentance?

2. If John's baptism wasn't the final baptism, why do you think God made John preach it and practice it?

Acts 16

14 One of those listening was a woman named Lydia, a dealer in purple
cloth from the city of Thyatira, who was a worshipper of God. The Lord
opened her heart to respond to Paul's message. 15 When she and the mem-
bers of her household were baptized, she invited us to her home. "If you
consider me a believer in the Lord," she said, "come and stay at my house."
And she persuaded us.

~

29 The jailer called for lights, rushed in and fell trembling before Paul and
Silas. 30 He then brought them out and asked, "Sirs, what must I do to be
saved?" 31 They replied, "Believe in the Lord Jesus, and you will be saved
— you and your household." 32 Then they spoke the word of the Lord to
him and to all the others in his house.

33 At that hour of the night the jailer took them and washed their wounds;
then immediately he and all his family were baptized. 34 The jailer brought
them into his house and set a meal before them; he was filled with joy
because he had come to believe in God — he and his whole family.

1. What did the jailer's belief in Jesus cause him to do that night?

2. Where did the jailer's joy come from?

3. Why does believing in God and obeying Him create such joy?

4. This passage talks about being saved, believing in Jesus, being baptized, and believing in God. How are they connected?

Acts 18

8 Crispus, the synagogue ruler, and his entire household believed in the
Lord; and many of the Corinthians who heard him [Paul] believed and
were baptized.

~

24 Meanwhile a Jew named Apollos, a native of Alexandria, came
to Ephesus. He was a learned man, with a thorough knowledge of the
Scriptures. 25 He had been instructed in the way of the Lord, and he
spoke with great fervor and taught about Jesus accurately, though he knew
only the baptism of John. 26 He began to speak boldly in the synagogue.
When Priscilla and Aquila heard him, they invited him to their home and
explained to him the way of God more adequately.

1. What do you think Priscilla and Aquila explained to Apollos?

2. This is the third or fourth passage in the Bible that mentions belief and baptism in the same sentence. How would you describe the interrelationship between belief and baptism?

Acts 19

1 Paul took the road through the interior and arrived at Ephesus. There he
found some disciples 2 and asked them, "Did you receive the Holy Spirit
when [or after] you believed?" They answered, "No, we have not even
heard that there is a Holy Spirit."

3 So Paul asked, "Then what baptism did you receive?" "John's baptism,"
they replied. 4 Paul said, "John's baptism was a baptism of repentance. He
told the people to believe in the one coming after him, that is, in Jesus."

5 On hearing this, they were baptized into [or in] the name of the Lord
Jesus. 6 When Paul placed his hands on them, the Holy Spirit came on
them, and they spoke in tongues [or other languages] and prophesied. 7
There were about twelve men in all.

1. Is Jesus' baptism a baptism of repentance as well?

2. Why/Why not?

3. What is repentance?

Acts 22

4 I (Paul) persecuted the followers of this Way to their death, arresting both
men and women and throwing them into prison, 5 as also the high priest
and all the Council can testify. I even obtained letters from them to their
brothers in Damascus, and went there to bring these people as prisoners to
Jerusalem to be punished. 6 "About noon as I came near Damascus, suddenly a bright light from heaven flashed around me. 7 I fell to the ground
and heard a voice say to me, 'Saul! Saul! Why do you persecute me?'

8 'Who are you, Lord?' I asked. 'I am Jesus of Nazareth, whom you are
persecuting,' he replied. 9 My companions saw the light, but they did not
understand the voice of him who was speaking to me.

10 "'What shall I do, Lord?' I asked. "'Get up,' the Lord said, 'and go into
Damascus. There you will be told all that you have been assigned to do.'
11 My companions led me by the hand into Damascus, because the bril-
liance of the light had blinded me. 12 "A man named Ananias came to see
me. He was a devout observer of the law and highly respected by all the
Jews living there. 13 He stood beside me and said, 'Brother Saul, receive
your sight!' And at that very moment I was able to see him. 14 "Then he
said: 'The God of our fathers has chosen you to know his will and to see
the Righteous One and to hear words from his mouth. 15 You will be his
witness to all men of what you have seen and heard. 16 And now what are
you waiting for? Get up, be baptized and wash your sins away, calling on
his name.'"

1. What two things was Paul told to do to wash his sins away?

   a. ____

   b. ____

2. How soon, after believing in Jesus, was Paul baptized?

   ____

3. This is the first verse where someone is instructed to "call upon the name of the Lord." Why is this instruction included here and not in every instance where people are being taught about baptism?

   ____

   ____

   ____

   ____

   ____

4. What does it mean to call upon the name of the Lord?

   ____

   ____

   ____

   ____

   ____

the letters

A collection of all the passages in
the Letters that mention baptism.

Romans 6

3 Or don't you know that all of us who were baptized into Christ Jesus
were baptized into his death? 4 We were therefore buried with him through
baptism into death in order that, just as Christ was raised from the dead
through the glory of the Father, we too may live a new life.

5 If we have been united with him like this in his death, we will certainly
also be united with him in his resurrection. 6 For we know that our old self
was crucified with him so that the body of sin might be rendered powerless
that we should no longer be slaves to sin — 7 because anyone who has died
has been freed from sin. 8 Now if we died with Christ, we believe that we
will also live with him.

1. When does your new life begin (v. 4)?

____

____

____

____

____

2. What is the connection between baptism and Jesus' death and resurrection?

____

____

____

____

____

1 Corinthians 1

11 My brothers, some from Chloe's household have informed me that there
are quarrels among you. 12 What I mean is this: One of you says, "I follow
Paul"; another, "I follow Apollos"; another, "I follow Peter"; still another,
"I follow Christ."

13 Is Christ divided? Was Paul crucified for you? Were you baptized into
[or in; also in verse 15] the name of Paul? 14 I am thankful that I did not
baptize any of you except Crispus and Gaius, 15 so no-one can say that
you were baptized into my name. 16 (Yes, I also baptized the household of
Stephanas; beyond that, I don't remember if I baptized anyone else.)

17 For Christ did not send me to baptize, but to preach the gospel — not
with words of human wisdom, lest the cross of Christ be emptied of its
power.

18 For the message of the cross is foolishness to those who are perishing, but
to us who are being saved it is the power of God.

1. Is Paul diminishing the value of baptism because he didn't personally baptize many people in Corinth?

1 Corinthians 10

1 For I do not want you to be ignorant of the fact, brothers, that our fore-
fathers were all under the cloud and that they all passed through the sea. 2
They were all baptized into Moses in the cloud and in the sea. 3 They all
ate the same spiritual food 4 and drank the same spiritual drink; for they
drank from the spiritual rock that accompanied them, and that rock was
Christ.

5 Nevertheless, God was not pleased with most of them; their bodies were
scattered over the desert. 6 Now these things occurred as examples to keep
us from setting our hearts on evil things as they did.

1. What kind of baptism is Paul talking about here?

____

____

____

____

____

2. What does this verse reveal to us about our baptism today?

____

____

____

____

____

1 Corinthians 12

12 The body is a unit, though it is made up of many parts; and though all
its parts are many, they form one body. So it is with Christ. 13 For we were
all baptized by [or with; or in] one Spirit into one body — whether Jews
or Greeks, slave or free — and we were all given the one Spirit to drink.

1 Corinthians 15

29 Now if there is no resurrection, what will those do who are baptized for the dead? If the dead are not raised at all, why are people baptized for them?

1. What does baptism have to do with us getting into the body (God's church) according to Paul in 1 Corinthians 12?

2. Thoughts/Notes

Galatians 3

26 You are all sons of God through faith in Christ Jesus, 27 for all of you
who were baptized into Christ have clothed yourselves with Christ.

28 There is neither Jew nor Greek, slave nor free, male nor female, for
you are all one in Christ Jesus. 29 If you belong to Christ, then you are
Abraham's seed, and heirs according to the promise.

1. How are becoming "sons of God," faith, and baptism interconnected in this passage?

2. Paul says we are baptized into Christ. List some other verses that share additional details of how we get into Christ.

Ephesians 4

[4] There is one body and one Spirit — just as you were called to one hope
when you were called — [5] one Lord, one faith, one baptism; [6] one God
and Father of all, who is over all and through all and in all.

Colossians 2

[9] For in Christ all the fullness of the Deity lives in bodily form, [10] and you
have been given fullness in Christ, who is the Head over every power and
authority. [11] In him you were also circumcised, in the putting off of the
sinful nature, [or the flesh] not with a circumcision done by the hands of
men but with the circumcision done by Christ, [12] having been buried with
him in baptism and raised with him through your faith in the power of
God, who raised him from the dead.

1. How many baptisms are there according to Ephesians 4:5?

___

2. If there is only one baptism, how does that fit with how we are baptized in water and Jesus baptizing us with the Holy Spirit and with fire, which appears to be two baptisms?

___

___

___

___

___

3. What does Colossians 2 tell you about baptism?

___

___

___

___

___

Hebrews 6

1 Therefore let us leave the elementary teachings about Christ and go on to
maturity, not laying again the foundation of repentance from acts that lead
to death, and of faith in God, 2 instruction about baptisms, the laying on
of hands, the resurrection of the dead, and eternal judgment. 3 And God
permitting, we will do so.

1 Peter 3

18 For Christ died for sins once for all, the righteous for the unrighteous,
to bring you to God. He was put to death in the body but made alive by
the Spirit, 19 through whom also he went and preached to the spirits in
prison 20 who disobeyed long ago when God waited patiently in the days
of Noah while the ark was being built. In it only a few people, eight in all,
were saved through water, 21 and this water symbolizes baptism that now
saves you also — not the removal of dirt from the body but the response of
a good conscience towards God. It saves you by the resurrection of Jesus
Christ, 22 who has gone into heaven and is at God's right hand — with
angels, authorities and powers in submission to him.

1. Since we're instructed to (eventually) leave behind the (elementary) Bible topics listed in Hebrews 6, what topics could we study to help us go on to maturity?

2. According to 1 Peter 3, what does baptism do for us?

may God bless you

and keep you;

the Lord make his face

shine on you

and be gracious to you;

the Lord turn his face

toward you and

give you peace.

conclusion

Final Comments

You have just read all the passages in the New Testament about baptism. So, what do you think? What did you learn? How has your perspective on baptism strengthened? How has it shifted?

Baptism is clearly a very important step in every believer's walk and has a strong spiritual significance. I encourage you not to just sit on this knowledge, but to act on it. Jesus Himself tells us to be doers of the Word, not merely hearers of it. If you've never been baptized and you believe in Jesus, then it's time to follow the biblical example and do so. If you have already been baptized by immersion, congratulations on fulfilling God's commands regarding baptism.

May God bless you and keep you; the Lord make his face shine on you and be gracious to you; the Lord turn his face toward you and give you peace.

appendix

The Greek Words for Baptism

WHAT ARE THE GREEK WORDS FOR BAPTISM?

There are 4 words related to baptism in the New Testament.

1. ***baptizō***

   This verb occurs 77 times in 64 verses.

   It means *to dip, immerse; to cleanse or purify by washing; to administer the rite of baptism, to baptize* (Acts 22:16).

2. ***baptisma***

   This noun occurs 19 times.

   It means *immersion; baptism, ordinance of baptism* (Mt.3:7, Rom.6:4).

3. ***baptistēs***

   This noun occurs 12 times and always refers to John the Baptist ("Baptizer") and means *one who baptizes, a baptist* (Mt.3:1).

4. ***baptismos***

   This noun occurs 4 times and means *an act of dipping or immersion: a baptism* (Mk.7:4, Col.2:12, Heb.6:2).

These words have been derived from the NA28 Greek text. All definitions are taken from *The New Analytical Greek Lexicon by W.J. Perschbacher.*

Topical Index

KEY TOPICS ASSOCIATED WITH BAPTISM

Each of these topics are mentioned in the same passage as baptism.

BELIEF / FAITH

CHURCH

CONFESSION

FORGIVENESS (OF SINS)

See also Sin and Salvation

HOLY SPIRIT

Matthew 3:11, 16

Matthew 28:19

Acts 1:5

Acts 2:38

Acts 8:15-18

Acts 10:47

Acts 11:15-16

Acts 19:1-6

IN THE NAME OF

Matthew 28:19

Acts 2:38

Acts 8:16

Acts 10:43, 48

Acts 19:5

Acts 22:16

Galatians 3:27

JOY / REJOICING

Acts 8:39

Acts 16:34

REPENTANCE

Matthew 3:11

Mark 1:4

Luke 3:3

Acts 2:38

Acts 13:24

Acts 19:3

Colossians 2:11-12

SALVATION

Mark 16:16

John 3:5

Acts 11:18

Acts 16:30-33

Romans 6:5

1 Corinthians 1:18

1 Peter 3:20-21

See also Forgiveness and Sin

SIN

Matthew 3:6

Mark 1:4-5

Luke 3:3

Acts 2:38

Acts 10:43

Acts 22:16

Romans 6:6-7

Colossians 2:11-12

1 Peter 3:18

See also Repentance and Forgiveness

WATER

Matthew 3:11, 16

John 3:5, 23

Acts 1:5

Acts 8:36-39

Acts 10:47

Acts 11:16

1 Peter 3:20-21

www.ingramcontent.com/pod-product-compliance
Lightning Source LLC
Chambersburg PA
CBHW071908020426
42331CB00010B/2718
* 9 7 9 8 9 9 0 1 6 7 6 0 5 *